21ST Century Skills **INNOVATION LIBRARY**

Disruptors in Tech

Movies and Music

Martin Gitlin

Published in the United States of America by Cherry Lake Publishing
Ann Arbor, Michigan
www.cherrylakepublishing.com

Reading Adviser: Marla Conn, MS, Ed., Literacy specialist, Read-Ability, Inc.

Photo Credits: ©Vladimir Sukhachev/Shutterstock.com, cover, 1 ; ©DeskGraphic/Shutterstock.com, cover, 1; ©Historic American Buildings Survey/Library of Congress/Control No. pa2993, 5; ©Vic Lab/Shutterstock.com, 6; ©hogy/Shutterstock.com, 7; ©Proxima Studio/Shutterstock.com, 8; ©Twin Design/Shutterstock.com, 11; ©Rawpixel.com/Shutterstock.com, 12, 26; ©franviser/Shutterstock.com, 13; ©Muhd Imran Ismail/Shutterstock.com, 14; ©Benjamin Clapp/Shutterstock.com, 17; ©Jasni/Shutterstock.com, 18; ©aradaphotography/Shutterstock.com, 20; © David Molina/Dreamstime, 23; ©LumineImages/Shutterstock.com, 24

Graphic Element Credits: ©Ohn Mar/Shutterstock.com, back cover, multiple interior pages; ©Dmitrieva Katerina/Shutterstock.com, back cover, multiple interior pages; ©advent/Shutterstock.com, back cover, front cover, multiple interior pages; ©Visual Generation/Shutterstock.com, multiple interior pages; ©anfisa focusova/Shutterstock.com, front cover, multiple interior pages; ©Babich Alexander/Shutterstock.com, back cover, front cover, multiple interior pages

Library of Congress Cataloging-in-Publication Data

Names: Gitlin, Marty, author.
Title: Movies and music / by Martin Gitlin.
Description: Ann Arbor : Cherry Lake Publishing, [2019] | Series: Disruptors in tech | Includes bibliographical references and index.
Identifiers: LCCN 2019005995 | ISBN 9781534147560 (hardcover) | ISBN 9781534148994 (pdf) | ISBN 9781534150423 (pbk.) | ISBN 9781534151857 (hosted ebook)
Subjects: LCSH: Motion picture industry–Technological innovations–Juvenile literature | Internet entertainment–Juvenile literature. | Music and technology–Juvenile literature. | Sound recording industry–Technological innovations–Juvenile literature.
Classification: LCC PN1994.5 .G58 2019 | DDC 384/.8–dc23
LC record available at https://lccn.loc.gov/2019005995

Printed in the United States of America
Corporate Graphics

Martin Gitlin has written more than 150 educational books. He also won more than 45 awards during his 11-year career as a newspaper journalist. Gitlin lives in Cleveland, Ohio.

Table of Contents

CHAPTER ONE

Theaters and Record Shops

Lines at theaters stretched around the block in the summer of 1975. Millions of Americans waited hours to buy tickets to see a movie about a killer shark. It was called *Jaws*.

The flick became known as the first summer "blockbuster." It earned more money at that time than any film in history.

Those yearning to see it had to visit the **cinema**. They had no other choices. That changed in the 1980s when people gained an option. Video stores, such as Blockbuster and other chains, opened, allowing people to rent movies on cassette tapes called VHS. Films could now be watched from the comfort of home.

There were still no DVDs. There was no Netflix. There was no streaming. Those who missed a movie playing at a theater had to hope it would eventually show up at a video store. Or it might appear on television. If neither happened, they were out of luck!

The first movies in the 1890s were silent and were only about a minute long!

The first vinyl records, made between 1898 and the 1950s, were called "78s" because they played at a speed of about 78 revolutions per minute.

Music fans also had to leave home to find what they wanted. They had one option in the 1960s and earlier. During that time, the music they heard on the radio was only available on records. They could visit a music store and buy a record. Then in the mid-1960s, 8-track tapes came along. Cassette tapes and compact discs (CDs) followed. But one could not purchase music from home.

Blockbuster was the king of video stores. But **digital downloading** and streaming all but wiped it out. By early 2019, only one Blockbuster remained in the world. It is in Bend, Oregon.

The film used to project *Titanic* (1997) onto a theater's movie screen was over 3 miles (5 kilometers) long. That's a lot of film!

Many critics complain that the sound and picture quality of songs and movies are worse when streamed versus when played on a vinyl or DVD.

Hello, Internet

The online world changed everything. Napster was the first file-sharing service to allow music fans to download copies of songs. In the short time Napster was around, about 80 million users easily obtained a wide variety of songs for free.

Online music stores such as iTunes and Google Play gave people legal options. The market opened further with the creation of streaming platforms that let users download music to listen to later without the internet. Companies such as Apple Music, Pandora, and Spotify let **subscribers** download any song or CD to a variety of devices for a monthly fee.

Much has changed since the turn of the 21st century. And **technology** promises many more changes in the future.

Birth of the Multiplex

Nearly every American theater into the 1970s had only one screen. So only one movie could be shown at a time. The advent of indoor shopping malls that decade started a trend toward **multiplex** movie houses. Today, almost all theaters boast many screens with multiple film offerings.

One man was ahead of his time. That was Stanley H. Durwood. He owned theaters in Kansas City, Missouri. In the 1950s, attendance at his theaters dropped when patrons began staying home to watch a new invention called television. His theater became so empty that he closed the balcony so he would not have to pay another usher.

Durwood realized that he could draw more patrons if he offered two movies at once. He built the first multiplex at the West Parkway Shopping Center. It opened on July 12, 1963. It aired a film that remains a classic, titled *The Great Escape*, on both screens. But soon his theater was showing two different movies on the separate screens. The multiplex was officially born.

CHAPTER TWO

Movies Without Going to the Movies

On April 14, 1998, a tiny California company launched a website called Netflix.com. It opened with only about 1,000 film titles to rent. But it started a revolution in the movie industry.

Netflix Killed the Video Store

The death of the video store was not far behind. No longer were movie fans forced to drive to Blockbuster to get the selection they wanted. They could instead cruise the **virtual** aisles and order their film of choice. The DVD would be waiting in their mailbox two or three days later.

Netflix quickly became the king of the movie video business. But it had to change with the times. It needed to compete with companies such as Amazon Prime and Hulu, which were streaming movies and TV shows directly onto subscribers' computers. Netflix launched an on-demand

Netflix has collected data about its users, including what movies they rent, since 2000. They use this information to recommend other movies.

streaming service in 2007. Three years later, Netflix had more than 20 million subscribers.

People could watch whatever movies they wanted whenever they wanted. They could also stream their favorite television shows. Some even ditched cable for on-demand options. TV ratings and attendance at movie theaters dropped.

One reason for the success of Netflix was that it began recommending movies to its subscribers. It based its recommendations on the movie tastes of each customer. These recommendations were based on the types of movies and TV shows that customers had previously streamed.

As of 2016, over 700 million hours of video content has been streamed on Hulu.

Keeping Up with the Competition

As the years passed, the competition became more intense. Netflix, Amazon Prime, and Hulu eventually began producing their own movies and TV programs.

Hollywood producers were taking no chances. They placed into theaters only movies that could draw crowds. Included were superhero flicks and sequels to *Star Wars* and *Batman*. Meanwhile, Netflix was earning a reputation for taking risks on unusual small-budget films. The company believed that customers—who could watch a movie with a few clicks—were also willing to take chances.

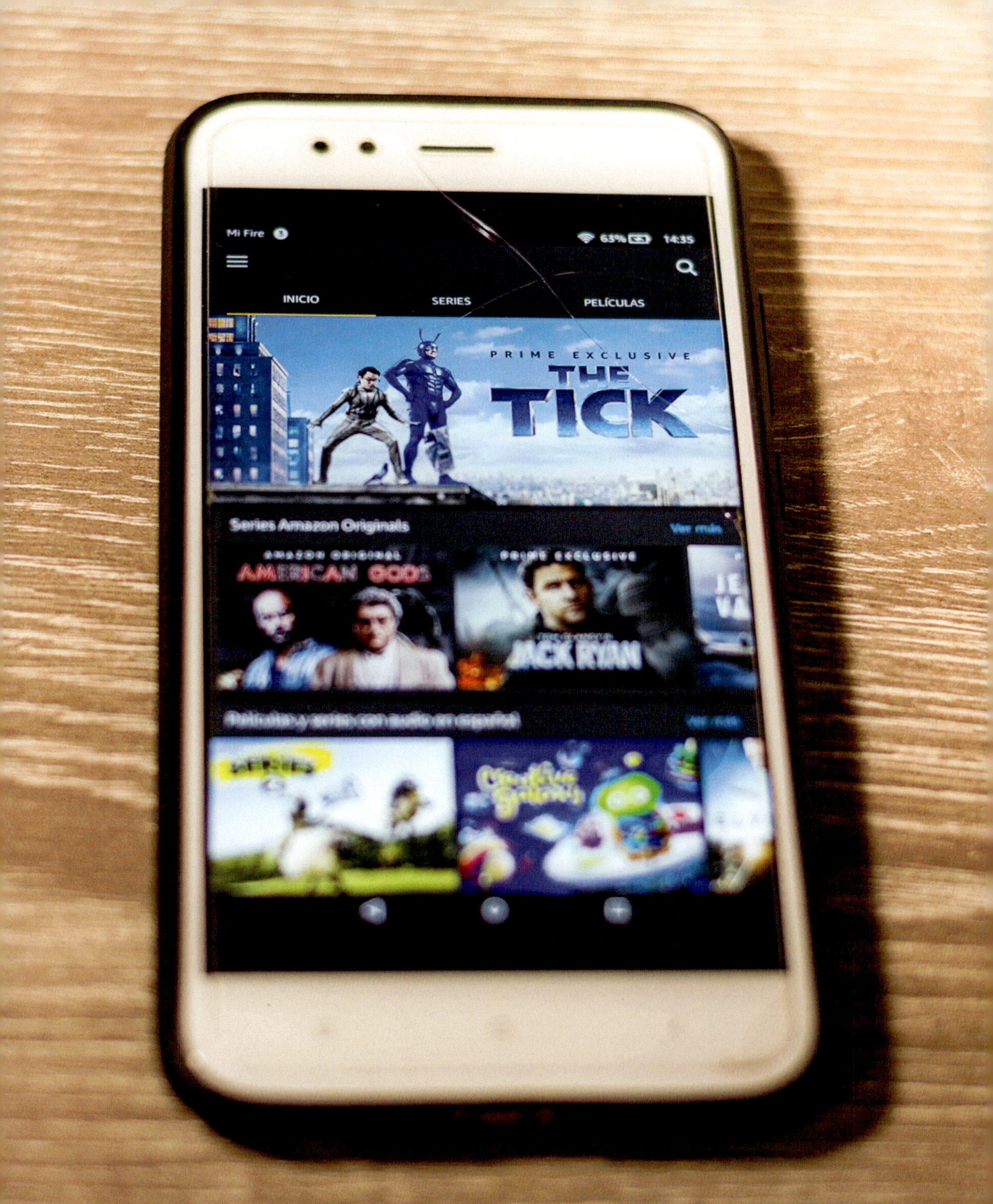

Amazon launched their video streaming service in 2011.

As of 2018, people in Saudi Arabia watch the most online video content compared to any other country, when including sites like YouTube.

Movie streaming services have not been content to attract only American audiences. More than half of Netflix subscribers live outside the United States. Companies such as Netflix, Amazon Prime, and Hulu continue to grow. And the number of patrons in theaters continues to shrink. These are trends that might never change.

The Rise of Hulu

Netflix has remained the top choice for movie streamers. But Hulu has gained great popularity. It topped 20 million subscribers in 2018. That was nearly a 20 percent increase over the last three months of 2017.

Hulu also took away some business from its rival. It signed a deal with DreamWorks Animation for access to the studio's old and new movies starting in 2019. DreamWorks had been developing shows for Netflix that featured popular characters from films such as *Shrek* and *How to Train Your Dragon*.

Hulu found success in the United States by offering live television in addition to streaming. Hulu uses its TV presence to stream channels from Disney, Fox, and NBC, which Netflix doesn't do. That put Hulu in a better position to compete against cable TV networks.

Hulu has also begun showing original movies. But its most successful original effort has been a television series called *The Handmaid's Tale*. Based on a 1985 book, the show was launched in 2017.

CHAPTER THREE

The Battle for Music Fans

While Netflix has dominated the movie streaming market, no dominant force has emerged in the music streaming market. Apple Music, Spotify, and Tidal have fought to win over music fans.

Convenience over Quality

There is one drawback to music streaming, and that is a lower quality sound. Streamed music is simply not as sharp as music on CDs, records, and digital downloads. But listeners are willing to trade quality for convenience. Streaming services feature a huge number of songs that are easy to find.

The streaming trend to play every song from one album helped British singer Ed Sheeran. Every song from his album titled *Divide* occupied the first 16 spots on the streaming charts in 2017.

Many claim Pandora as the first real pioneer in streaming music.

Music Industry Interrupted

The dominance of streaming has changed the music industry. An artist used to release a new song that would spend months battling other songs on the market. Streaming music results in music fans buying individual songs from an album released by an artist, instead of buying the entire album.

While streaming is great for fans, it sometimes isn't so great for the artist. Free streaming services, like Pandora and Spotify, often make money through advertisements. A portion of this money goes to the artists. For most artists, the money they receive from streaming services isn't as much as they would have received if more people purchased their albums.

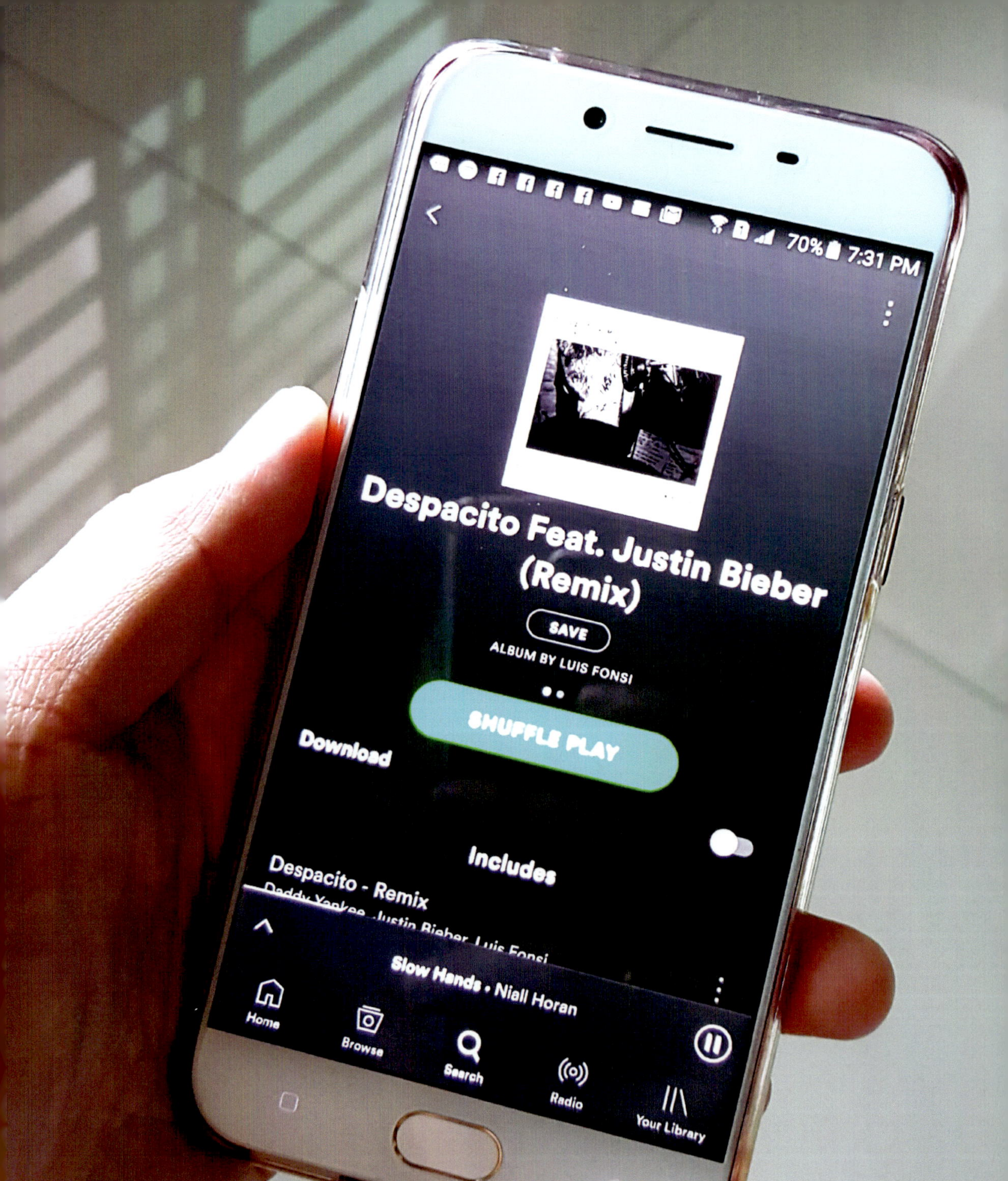

According to a media studies professor, in order for a songwriter to make minimum wage in California, his or her song must be streamed about 4 million times on Spotify!

Artists Protest

Popular singer-songwriter Taylor Swift protested this lack of income by pulling her music off Spotify and Apple. Spotify responded by placing her music only on its paid service rather than its free service.

Artists' threats of refusing to place their music on these services have had an effect. Companies such as Apple Music and Spotify have pushed to convince artists to sign deals only with them. This ensures that music fans must subscribe to their services to hear those artists. As a result, fans can only stream the Frank Ocean album *Blonde* through Apple Music and Spotify. And the Beyoncé album *Lemonade* can only be streamed through Tidal.

The impact of streaming on music and movies has been powerful. Neither industry will ever be the same.

As of 2018, more people in the United States streamed music on Apple Music than any other service.

Great Spot for Spotify

Spotify is one of the most popular music streaming services in the world. It had more than 200 million active users by the middle of 2018. Among them were 87 million paid subscribers. They are attracted to the **playlist** of about 30 million songs. Spotify offers unlimited access to those tunes for one monthly fee.

The songs on Spotify are available on nearly every platform. Fans have been signing up at an incredible pace. The number of its subscribers more than doubled from September 2016 to June 2018.

The company was born in Sweden in 2006. It soon moved its base to London, England. Spotify started offering streaming services in 2008. After losing money that year, it began offering free accounts and launched on the Apple App Store. Spotify opened to American fans 3 years later. It became available on Android smartphones in 2012.

Spotify took off. It had 10 million subscribers by May 2014 and has added subscribers ever since. Its jump of 13 million in the first half of 2018 was the largest in the history of the company.

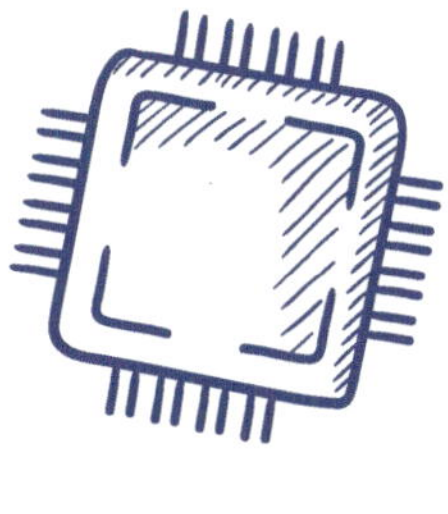

CHAPTER FOUR

The Domination of Streaming

The numbers tell the whole story. Streaming has taken over. It has changed the music business more than it has the movie industry. But it has impacted both greatly.

Money Made and Lost in Music

The Recording Industry Association of America (RIAA) released telling statistics in 2018. Three-fourths of all music **revenue** during the first half of that year were earned through streaming. Digital downloads and physical purchases of CDs and albums accounted for nearly all the rest. Money earned from streaming had already taken a huge leap from 2017. This shows how quickly and completely streaming has taken over the music industry.

According to experts, approximately 1 million plays on Spotify earns an artist about $5,000 and on Pandora about $1,472.

Many people claim that streaming movies online is better than watching in the theaters.

One cannot imagine a return to the old days. Some music fans love the sound of albums and still buy them for their record players. Music CDs have suffered a far worse fate. Sales of CDs dropped 90 percent after peaking in 2000.

Money Made and Lost in Movies

There is no doubt that Netflix dominates the movie streaming industry. Netflix boasted more than 117 million subscribers worldwide in 2017. It also earned $11 billion that year. But it has worthy competitors. Amazon Prime and Hulu are quickly gaining popularity among movie streamers.

Movie theaters attendance dropped to a 25-year low in 2017, with only a little over 1.2 million movie tickets sold in the United States and Canada. Between 1999 and 2004, the average number of movie tickets sold was over 1.5 million!

One of the most popular stores from which to purchase CDs had been Best Buy. But the rise of streaming music and collapse of CD sales caused Best Buy to make a tough decision. The company stopped selling music CDs in 2018.

Almost half of the people who buy vinyl records are under 25 years old.

What Do You Prefer?

Some believe that streaming is a matter of convenience over quality. They claim that music sounds better on albums or CDs, but people prefer the ease of streaming music. Some feel that watching streamed films on TV cannot compare to seeing them on large theater screens. But people would still rather save money on tickets and popcorn and watch them at home.

Technology will continue to evolve. And that means streaming will continue to make life easier for music and movie lovers.

Vinyl Is Revived

Old-fashioned vinyl records had nearly died out even before streaming. The CD industry had all but killed sales of record albums by the year 2000.

But something unexpected happened. Albums began making a huge comeback. Those who love the crisp sound of music from vinyl started buying records and record players again. Record sales grew for 11 straight years from 2006 to 2017. More than 14 million albums were sold in the United States in 2017. That was the highest number since at least 1991.

Retail stores such as Amazon and Urban Outfitters thrived selling vinyl. Classic rock music sold very well. The most purchased record in 2017 was produced by a group that broke up in 1970. It was the landmark *Sgt. Pepper's Lonely Hearts Club Band* album by the Beatles. The album celebrated its 50th anniversary in 2017.

Timeline

1889
German-born Emile Berliner demonstrates the first early concept of the record player to a toy company.

1905
The Nickelodeon in Pittsburgh, Pennsylvania, opens as the first public movie theater in the United States.

1981
The first pop album is transformed into a compact disc (CD).

1985
The first Blockbuster video store opens.

1993
The Internet Underground Music Archive provides the first free online music service.

1998
Netflix's launch begins having an impact on the movie industry.

2005
Pandora radio starts providing free music with ads or paid subscriptions.

2008
Spotify begins its streaming service.

2011
Spotify becomes available to American consumers.

2015
Apple Music gives consumers another streaming alternative.

Learn More

Books

Burgan, Michael. *Spotify, Pandora, and Streaming Music.* Broomall, PA: Mason Crest, 2018.

Green, Sara. *Netflix.* Minneapolis, MN: Bellwether Media, 2018.

Websites

KidzSearch

www.kidzsearch.com/radio.html
This site provides free online radio stations and music videos.

Netflix Children and Family Movies

https://www.netflix.com/browse/genre/783
This Netflix page provides movie choices best suited for kids and their families.

Glossary

cinema (SIN-uh-muh) movie theater

digital (DIJ-ih-tuhl) relating to computer technology

downloading (DOUN-lohd-ing) transferring data from a computer to a smaller device

multiplex (MUHL-tee-pleks) movie theater with more than one screen

playlist (PLAY-list) all songs to choose from

retail (REE-tayl) the business of selling things directly to customers for their own use

revenue (REV-uh-noo) income produced by a given source

subscribers (suhb-SKRIBE-urz) people who pay for a particular service

technology (tek-NAH-luh-jee) use of science to solve problems

virtual (VUR-choo-uhl) artificial environment experienced through sights and sounds provided by a computer

Index